If only
YOU would
ASK

A Guide to Spending Quality Time
With the Elderly

An enjoyable resource for
Adult Children, Grandchildren, Friends, Caregivers, Clergy,
Therapists, and Volunteers

Eileen Opatz Berger and Joan Berger Bachman

Published by Wheatmark®
2030 East Speedway Boulevard, Suite 106
Tucson, Arizona 85719 USA
www.wheatmark.com

ISBN: 978-1-62787-463-2
LCCN: 2016956009

This book is dedicated to
all those willing to take the time
to ask the questions

"*The best classroom of all is at the feet of the elderly.*"

—Andy Rooney

Contents

Contents

Contents

Preface

How this book came about

My father-in-law, Bill, died five years ago. He insisted on staying in his home until the end. Winters in Minnesota are long, cold, and lonely, especially for someone who is afraid to venture out. In his last months, I felt compelled to drive the one hundred miles to visit him. We would sit at his kitchen table, and I would tell him about what the kids were up to... and what I had been doing. His major topic of conversation was the rabbits he saw as he stared for hours out the back window of his house.

During this time, I shared with my mother how difficult visits with Bill were becoming. He had so little to share, and I wondered if the visits even mattered.

Not long after, Mom gave me a notebook filled with a list of questions. She suggested I try asking Bill some of these questions to make our visits more enjoyable. "Leave it on the counter," she advised. "The grandchildren might appreciate using the questions. I took the notebook over to Bill's house and meant to get started the next time we visited. That was the last time I spoke with Bill. And now he is gone, and so many questions remain unanswered.

Joan Berger Bachman, 2017

Everybody has a story! Everybody!

It is only by asking the right questions that we begin to uncover the richness of each person's journey. Aunt Helen and Uncle Joe might think that their life is not interesting. But the truth is, everybody's life is unique and of value. Everybody has experienced happiness, sadness, anger, and joy. And for sure, there is a story to go along with all of these feelings.

I visited a great aunt some years ago with my mother. I had never met her before this visit. At the time, I asked many questions concerning her growing up in pioneer Minnesota. She seemed delighted to answer them. Later that day, she said, "Nobody has ever asked me those questions." And her eyes filled up with tears. I know I went home impressed with this strong lady, and I know she felt happy, too. Using the questions in this book as a guide, I think you will have the same kind of experiences.

Eileen Opatz Berger, 2017

Introduction

Have you ever felt obliged to visit a relative or friend in a nursing home or retirement facility? How about someone in long-term care? For purposes of this introduction, we will refer to them as Uncle Joe and Aunt Helen. "I don't look forward to visiting Joe and Helen, but if I don't go, who will?" And then come the obligatory hours sitting at a bedside or next to a wheelchair making small talk about what you've been doing for the last week, how the kids are, or the weather. Joe and Helen have little to share as they haven't been out of the building or perhaps even out of their room. And so the hour crawls by, you kiss them goodbye, tell them to hang in there, and you'll see them next week. Leaving the building, you feel sorry that their life has been reduced to four walls, a television, and meals, and you wish you could do something to make the visit more enjoyable for them and, let's be honest, for yourself.

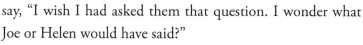

Has it ever happened that after someone you love dies, you say, "I wish I had asked them that question. I wonder what Joe or Helen would have said?"

Alex Haley wrote: "Every time an old person dies, it's like a library burning down. Ideas, memories, lessons, histories, dreams—all go with them. It is almost a complete erasure, except for the memories still alive in the hearts of the living. And in a generation or two, those memories will also be gone."

Most elderly will say they have done nothing out of the ordinary. Perhaps this is what Joe and Helen would say. However, everybody has a story! If we ask the right questions, if we are interested in finding out about this person with whom we sit, who knows what we might learn? In answering our questions, they will be reminded of events they may not have thought about for years

Whether you choose to write down what you hear is up to you. The goal of these questions is not to create an autobiography but to *uplift the spirit of the person sharing their story.* The hours will fly by, and you will go home looking forward to your next visit.

Why is this book important?

Across our world, in homes, apartments, long-term care facilities, nursing homes, hospitals, and hospices, thousands of elderly men and women are feeling isolated, lonely, and of no value. Although many may be genuinely loved by family and friends, visits become increasingly obligatory and one-sided. There is so little to talk about.

The purpose of *If Only You Would Ask* is to give children,

grandchildren, relatives, caregivers, and volunteers a way to spend enjoyable hours with the elderly. Senior citizens living in convalescent homes, retirement homes, or in their own homes will realize that they do have interesting stories to share, "if only someone would ask."

For whom is this book written?

This book is written for those who VISIT and SPEND TIME with the elderly, wherever they may live. The questions contained herein serve as a key to unlock stories and memories. It is in the telling of these stories that the elderly are reminded that they are valued people who have lived meaningful lives.

How does it work?

Each topic in *If Only You Would Ask* is organized as a two-page unit that includes a **Hook Question**, **Follow Up Questions**, and **Trigger Words**.

The Hook Question, bold and in a box, is fairly general in nature. In some cases, the hook may be all you need to spark an interesting conversation. If, however, the person to whom you are speaking is not able to remember an event or provide many details, **Follow Up Questions** are provided. Use as many or as few of the follow up questions as needed to keep the conversation flowing. Finally, across the top of each page you will see a stream of **Trigger Words**. Triggers provide additional prompts to unlock memories.

Sometimes an answer will include a word or phrase that leads the conversation in a different direction. When this is the case, go with it! The most important thing is that both you and the person with whom you are speaking are engaged in a topic of interest.

Starting the conversation

People you already know...

More than likely, the people you visit will be related or well-known to you; parents, grandparents, aunts, uncles, or friends. If so, an already established level of comfort and trust exists that allows for general conversation to flow freely, i.e. weather, food, and health. When you are having conversations with someone you already know, it is easier to talk to them about your sincere interest in finding out more about the many stories of their lives. You may even want to show them your copy of *If Only You Would Ask,* offering a brief overview of the many questions you are eager to ask them!

People you've never met...

There will, however, be people you visit whom you do not know well or perhaps not at all. When this is the case, introduce yourself as a volunteer visitor who would very much appreciate talking to them about their life. It will be up to you to establish a sincere level of interest in what the person has to say. Tell the person how much you would appreciate learning about their growing up years and the years that followed.

Once permission has been granted, begin with questions that are general and comfortable. *Where did you grow up? How long have you been living here?* A surefire way to begin a conversation is to comment on a craft you see in the room or a photo on the wall. Ask about it. More specific details will surface. It is at this point that you can choose to show them your copy of *If Only You Would Ask* and page through the chapters together. There very well may be a topic that calls out to them in some way. The rest is up to you!

If it happens that someone appears to be uncomfortable and/or reluctant to share on a certain topic, honor their feelings and move to another topic. A person should never feel that he/she is being interrogated.

Ending the conversation

Once your visit is over, consider leaving the book with the person you are visiting. In their quiet time, they may enjoy paging through the book, looking at the pictures, considering the many topics, and realizing just how much they really have to share.

Don't underestimate the power of listening!

It may seem a paradox in a book about conversation to emphasize listening. However, a good conversationalist is actually a good listener. All of us can be good listeners if we follow a few suggestions:

1. When one person looks directly at another person, is fully present to that person and listens with interest, something very special happens. That person feels valued.

2. A good listener follows the other's train of thought and asks questions to better understand what is being shared. It is like putting yourself in the other person's shoes.

3. When the conversation is open-ended and spontaneous, the speaker will be motivated to expand his/her thoughts and dig deeper into memories that may not have been tapped into for many years.

4. It is not the job of a good listener to offer solutions or a quick fix. The focus is on the telling!

5. A good listener is in no hurry to jump in and talk about him/herself. However, If sharing an example from your life encourages the conversation, all the better!

6. Silence will happen and that is OK. Topics that have

not been thought about for years may take time to recall. Give the person with whom you are visiting a few moments to gather their thoughts. Haven't we all been in situations where we wish we had said such and such but didn't think of it at the time!

7. Most probably, those asking the questions will have a cell phone in their pocket or purse. A word of advice: Turn off or silence your cell phone during all conversations! The person with whom you are speaking is your primary focus!

The order of questions is not important

If Only You Would Ask is a conversational resource. You may start at the beginning, the middle, or at the end of the book and work backwards! Turn to page 6 or page 26, or whatever page grabs your interest and get started. Begin with the **Hook**! If a particular follow-up question doesn't appear to generate much interest, find one that does! Don't hesitate to rephrase a question to ignite a memory.

And remember... HAVE FUN!!

In the Beginning

What do you remember about your grade school years?

1) How did you get to school? Did you carry a lunch?

2) Who was your favorite elementary school teacher?

3) What did you do during recess?

4) Was there a bully in your school?

5) Do you still maintain a friendship with a grade school friend?

6) As an elementary age student, what obstacles did you face?

7) What was a favorite song or game you remember?

8) Were your parents involved as leaders or coaches in your activities?

9) What are some happy memories from your grade school years?

2 🚲 Birth Order

How many brothers and sisters do you have? Which number child are you?

1)   How did you feel about growing up in a large family?

2)   How did you feel about growing up in a small family?

3)   In what ways did your parents treat older children differently than younger children? How did you feel about that?

4)   Which sibling caused you the most grief?

5)   To which sibling were you closest?

6)   How much competitiveness existed between siblings? How did this affect future relationships?

7)   Which of your siblings got the most attention? As a child? As an adult?

8)   Was an adoption story part of your growing up years?

9)   What impact did a special-needs child have on the family?

What is your earliest memory?

1) Imagine you are opening the door of the first house you remember. Walk in and describe what you see.

2) As a child, how much responsibility were you given?

3) Who raised you?

4) Were praise and affection part of your growing up?

5) Who was your best friend? What kinds of activities did you do together?

6) What were your favorite radio programs and TV shows?

7) How did your family spend weekends?

8) As a child, what obstacles did you overcome?

9) Did you cause your parents a lot of worry? In what ways?

10) In your growing up years, what do you wish had been different?

Describe the place where you grew up?
What did it look like?

1) Do you recall any significant buildings or landmarks?

2) Was it a welcoming community?

3) What was your favorite season of the year?

4) Were there specific summer or winter events you looked forward to?

5) Growing up, what chores were expected of you?

6) What were the major nationalities of people in your community?

7) Where did young people hang out?

8) How did most families earn a living?

9) What did you like best about the place where you grew up?

Growing up, what was a favorite family outing or vacation?

1) What did your family do for fun?

2) What are some of your best memories from family outings?

3) What do you recall about visits to your grandparents or aunts and uncles?

4) If you camped, did you ever have a scare from some wild animal or bad weather?

5) What is a funny story you recall from a family outing?

6) What historic sites, such as the White House or Gettysburg, did you visit?

7) From which family vacation did you learn a lot?

8) Was there a person, place, or image from a vacation that forever changed your life?

9) What vacations/outings have you enjoyed with your adult children and grandchildren?

10) What is a family trip you will never forget?

Friends   *Part-time Jobs*   *Proms*   *Homework*   *Sports*

On a scale of 1-10, how would you rate your high school years?

1) Describe your personality as a teen.

2) What was the hardest part about being a teenager?

3) Did a certain teacher/mentor have an impact on your life? Explain.

4) With whom did you hang out?

5) How did you feel about your parents?

6) What did you do to earn spending money?

7) How did your participation in a club or on a team impact your high school years?

8) Did a best friend in high school remain a life-long friend?

9) Did you ever get in trouble with the law?

10) What is the best thing you remember about high school?

College *Military* *Trade School* *Night School*

As a high school student, what types of jobs or careers did you consider?

1) As a young adult, what were your interests? What were your skills?

2) Did you have an option about continuing your education, or did you have to get a job?

3) What kind of higher education appealed to you?

4) How much support did you get from your parents?

5) Did you ever consider a religious vocation?

6) What were your greatest challenges in pursuing your dreams?

7) When did you consider yourself to be an adult?

8) Did you ever consider joining the military? If so, why?

9) As a student, did you ever have the opportunity to study abroad? How did this change your life?

10) What was one of the best decisions you made?

8

You Did What?

| Peace Corps | Prison Employee | Belly Dancer | Corn Detasseling |

> # What was one of the most unusual jobs you ever had?

1)   How did you find out about the job?

2)   How old were you when you took the job?

3)   Why were you hired?

4)   How long did you do the job?

5)   What did you like best about the job?

6)   What was the most difficult part of the job?

7)   What skills did you learn that may have helped you in the future?

8)   What positive memories do you still have from this experience?

9)   What was a memorable incident related to the job?

10)   Did you earn enough money at this job to support yourself?

So That's How It Happened!

What did you do to support yourself and your family?

1) How hard was it to get your first full-time job?

2) Did your first job turn out to be the job you wanted?

3) How did your education prepare you for your job?

4) What were your greatest job challenges?

5) What about your job gave you a sense of accomplishment?

6) By the time you retired, how many different jobs had you held? In how many places had you lived?

7) What was the highlight of your professional life?

8) Do you wish you had chosen a different path? Why didn't you make a change?

9) What advice would you give to a young person about choosing a career?

10  Dating

Blind   *On-Line*   *Chaperones*   *Going Dutch*

> # What was the hardest part about dating?

1) At what age did you start dating?

2) Where did you go on dates? What did you do?

3) Was dating encouraged/discouraged by your parents?

4) How did you meet the people you dated?

5) Describe your most memorable date.

6) On a date, who should pay?

7) How did you feel about blind dates?

8) How has dating changed over the years?

9) Can you share a story about someone who met their future husband/wife online?

Why did you get married when you did?

1) Do you believe in love at first sight?

2) How long did you date the person you married before he/she proposed? How did it happen?

3) What was it about your spouse/partner that made you want to get married? How old were you?

4) What were the most important qualities you looked for in a spouse? Do you still believe these are the most important qualities?

5) Describe your wedding day.

6) Where did you go on your honeymoon?

7) What was your hardest adjustment as a married person?

8) Have you been divorced? If so, what led to the breakup?

9) What advice would you give to a new mother-in-law, daughter-in-law, father-in-law, or son-in-law?

12 ☙ Parenting: Joys and Trials

Do you have children?
How many?

"Before the psychologist got married,
she had four theories about raising children.
Now she has four children and no theories."

—*Unknown*

1) Was there anything unusual or significant about your pregnancies?

2) What is the story behind your children's names?

3) How did you discipline your children?

4) How was your parenting different than the way you were parented?

5) Was it more challenging to raise daughters or sons?

6) How did a special-needs child impact your family?

7) What struggles did your children face, and how did you deal with them?

8) Describe a time you feared for the life of your child.

9) What has been the most difficult part of parenting?

10) What about parenting has brought you the most joy?

13 ❧ Starting Your Own Business

Why did you decide to start your own business?

"When you enjoy what you do,
it is like pouring nutrients into your soul."

— *Unknown*

28

1)   What was the most challenging part of starting your own business?

2)   What skills or interests led you to consider starting a business?

3)   Was there a friend or family member who helped you along the way?

4)   In what ways was your personality a good fit for the business you chose?

5)   What gave you the greatest feeling of accomplishment?

6)   What were the benefits of running your own business? What were the pitfalls?

7)   Did you consider going into business with a relative?

8)   What advice would you give to a young person looking to start a business?

9)   Would you pursue the same path if you had to do it over again?

Core Beliefs

How important has religion been in your life?

1) Growing up, how important was it to attend the church, the temple, or the mosque?

2) Who or what was instrumental in forming your religious beliefs?

3) What are the most important ceremonies or celebrations in your faith tradition?

4) How important were priests, ministers, or rabbis in your family?

5) Did you or a family member ever consider a religious vocation?

6) How have your ideas about religion changed since you were a teenager?

7) What challenges your faith?

8) What is your idea of an afterlife?

9) Can you share a favorite psalm or prayer?

10) When do you feel God's presence in your life?

How do you feel
about politics?

1)   Which political party do you support and why?

2)   What do you consider the most important qualities for someone running for political office?

3)   What politician(s) have you admired?

4)   Do you think it makes any difference for whom you vote?

5)   Did any of your relatives ever run for or hold public office?

6)   In what ways have you participated in the political process?

7)   If you were president, what would you do?

Citizens of other countries:

8)   What kind of government is practiced in your native country?

9)   If you could change one thing about your government, what would it be?

16
All About the Military

Separation   *Duty*   *Post Traumatic Stress*   *Disability*

> # Did you ever serve in the military?

1) Which branch of the military did you join? Why?

2) What do you remember about your basic training? Did you experience hazing?

3) Where were you deployed?

4) Were you ever in a situation where you felt your life was in danger?

5) Where was your favorite assignment?

6) What rank did you attain?

7) How long did you serve in the military?

8) How difficult was reentry into civilian life?

9) What are the benefits of a military career?

10) Would you encourage a family member to join the military?

17 ❦ Celebrations/ Holidays/Holy Days

Christmas   *Hanukah*   *Eid*   *Dwali*   *Chinese New Year*

What is your favorite holiday?

1) Does your family make a big deal about birthdays?

2) What is the most important celebration in your family?

3) What special foods are prepared for this special day?

4) Is religion part of the celebration?

5) Was the appearance of a jolly Santa part of your Christmas Eve?

6) What family traditions have been passed down from generation to generation?

7) Describe weddings in your family.

8) What was one of the happiest celebrations of your life?

9) Do you recall a holiday or celebration that didn't turn out the way you had hoped?

Health Related Issues

How would you describe your health?

Carved on a tombstone:
"I told you I was sick but did you believe me? Nooooo!"

—Unknown

1) How has your health impacted your life?

2) What do you do to stay healthy?

3) What kinds of surgeries have you had?

4) Did you ever feel your life was in danger due to an accident or a disease?

5) What health issues run in your family?

6) How have you coped with challenges to your health?

7) Can you share any home remedies?

8) What are your memorable experiences with a doctor or nurse?

9) Was there a time that you or someone you know experienced a medical miracle?

10) How do you feel about donating your organs?

Sports Related Activities

What are your favorite sports?

1)   When did your love for this sport begin?

2)   Who got you interested in this sport?

3)   How would you describe your commitment to this sport? (time/money/energy)

4)   How much danger was there in pursuing this sport?

5)   What was your greatest sports related accomplishment?

6)   Can you share a favorite hunting or fishing story?

7)   Where have you traveled to enjoy a sport?

8)   What was the scariest experience you had related to a sport?

9)   What athletes have you admired and why?

10)   What are your favorite sports teams?

All About Money

**How much money
does it take
to have a good life?**

1)   Do you enjoy spending money or saving money?

2)   How do you feel about paying with credit cards versus paying with cash?

3)   What is the best bargain you ever made at a thrift store or garage sale?

4)   Have you ever been scammed?

5)   How do you feel about purchasing a new versus a used car?

6)   How do you feel about renting versus buying?

7)   What is one of the best investments you ever made?

8)   What's the best advice you can give a young wage earner?

9)   When it comes to money, what have you learned?

All About the Arts

21 🦎 Art: Creation and Appreciation

Traditional   *Modern*   *Abstract*   *Impressionist*

When you visit an art museum, which exhibits do you most enjoy?

1) Do you have a favorite artist? Explain.

2) What kind of art do you own?

3) If you are an artist, what kind of art do you create?

4) What is your favorite subject matter?

5) Describe your favorite creation(s).

6) Did your parents encourage you to pursue this interest? Did you have a mentor?

7) How many hours each week do you spend doing your art?

8) Have you ever earned money with your art?

9) Do you think anyone can learn to draw or paint?

Music for the Soul

Classical   *Pop*   *Country*   *Rock 'n' Roll*   *Rap*

When you listen to music, what type of music do you prefer?

Note: Perhaps you can access a favorite song/artist on a device and listen to it together!

1) What about music do you enjoy most? Listening? Singing? Playing an instrument?

2) Over the years, who have been your favorite singers or musicians?

3) What is the best concert you have ever attended?

4) What instrument(s) do you play?

5) How did you choose this instrument?

6) How old were you when you began to take lessons?

7) Have you ever played an instrument in a band or an orchestra?

8) Have you ever written any original music?

9) Have you ever sung solos or belonged to a choir? Where?

10) How has your taste in music changed over the years?

23 ⚜ Theatre: "Break a Leg!"

Broadway   *Community*   *High School*   *Drama*   *Comedy*

When you go to the theatre, do you prefer musicals, comedies, or dramas?

1)　What have been some of your favorite productions?

2)　How often do you go to the theatre?

3)　Have you ever performed in a play? When? Where?

4)　What did you like best about being on the stage?

5)　Have you ever worked backstage? If so, what did you do?

6)　Have you ever been involved with theatre as a volunteer? What did you do?

7)　Who are your favorite actors?

8)　If you could play any role, what would it be?

9)　What is the best theatrical production you have ever seen?

How important is dancing in your life?

1) What kind of music makes you want to dance?

2) At what events are you most likely to dance?

3) Who taught you to dance?

4) Growing up, what kinds of dance lessons did you take?

5) How important were dance recitals?

6) Do you enjoy ballroom dancing? Which dances are your favorites?

7) Did you or your friends ever spend an evening dancing in a local ballroom or nightclub?

8) Can anyone learn to dance?

9) Why is it that some people, especially grown men, refuse to get out on the dance floor?

10) What do you think of programs like *Dancing With the Stars?*

Reaching Out

What is one of the best volunteer experiences you've ever had?

1) Why did you choose to volunteer for this particular organization?

2) Who are the people who benefit from this organization?

3) Growing up, did you ever belong to the Boy Scouts, Girl Scouts, 4H, Future Leaders of America, or some such group? What did you like best about this group? How did belonging to this group impact your life?

4) Have you ever worked with the homeless or those suffering from addictions?

5) Have you ever volunteered with immigrants?

6) What kinds of experiences have you had regarding people with special needs?

7) Have you ever worked with inmates or incarcerated persons?

8) Which service club or organization would you advise a young person to join?

Life's Little Pleasures

What kind of movies do you like?

1) What makes a movie memorable for you?

2) Who are your favorite actors?

3) What are some of the best movies you have ever seen?

4) What is one of the funniest movies you've ever watched?

5) When you sit down to watch TV, what channels or types of programs do you watch?

6) What are some of your favorite TV programs?

7) Are you a person that remembers all the lyrics to songs learned years ago?

8) What kinds of albums, CDs or sheet music did you buy?

9) Do you have a special song that brings back good memories?

Love of Reading...

Science Fiction   *Mysteries*   *Fiction*   *Nonfiction*   *Cookbooks*

How important has reading been in your life?

*"The more that you read, the more things you will
know. The more that you learn,
the more places you'll go."*

—*Dr. Seuss*

1) What type of books do you read most?

2) How do you decide which books to read?

3) How do you feel about reading a book on a Kindle?

4) How do you feel about listening to audio books or books on tape?

5) Do you enjoy owning your own books or borrowing them from a library? Why?

6) Have you ever belonged to a book club? What did you enjoy about belonging to this club?

7) What is a book that you will never forget?

8) Who are your favorite authors?

9) Growing up, how important was reading in your home?

10) What do you enjoy most about reading?

28 Hobbies and Activities

What hobbies or activities consume many hours of your time?

1) What do you enjoy most about your hobby?

2) For how long has this hobby been part of your life?

3) Does your hobby provide a source of income?

4) Have you ever received recognition for your hobby?

5) How do you share your hobby with others?

6) What skill do you have that may surprise others to learn?

7) What kinds of items do you create?

8) What kind of games do you enjoy? Cards? Board Games? Bingo?

9) Do you enjoy gambling? If so, what type of gambling? Casinos? Horse Racing? Sports Teams?

10) Have you ever won (or lost) a sizable amount of money from gambling?

Have you ever collected something?

1)   Who first got you interested in collecting?

2)   How valuable is your collection?

3)   Where is a good place to find items for your collection?

4)   How much time do you spend working on your collection?

5)   What is the best part of having a collection? What is the most difficult?

6)   Have you attended meetings to compare and trade items?

7)   How much expense is required to pursue your hobby?

8)   What is the strangest collection you've ever heard of?

30 ⌘
Travels Near and Far

If you could travel anywhere, where would it be? Why?

*"The world is a great book and they
who never stir from home read but a page."*
—Robb

1) Has travel been a priority for you?

2) Have you had many opportunities to travel? If so, explain.

3) How did a study/work abroad program impact your life?

4) Which type of trip do you enjoy more: biking, hiking, cruising, food tasting, or academic?

5) What has been your favorite destination in the US? Abroad?

6) Did you ever have a scare while traveling?

7) What was the most difficult part of traveling in a foreign country?

8) Have you ever been far away from home and run into someone you know?

Relationships

31 ✂ Ancestors

> ## Tell me about your ancestors.
> ## Where did they come from?

1) Why did your ancestors choose to settle where they did?

2) How old were your ancestors when they immigrated to the US?

3) How did your ancestors support themselves?

4) Growing up, was a language other than English spoken in your home?

5) Among your ancestors, was there someone especially memorable? (musician, inventor, politician.)

6) Have you ever visited the country from which your ancestors came? What surprised you?

7) What is a favorite memory of a grandparent?

8) What cultural traditions does your family continue to enjoy?

Who are the most important people in your life?

*Special Others: Many people who have not raised their own children have played loving roles in the lives of other children. Use these questions to talk about these relationships.

1) Tell me about your children. Where do they live? What kind of work do they do? How often do you see each other?

2) What events have helped you stay connected with your children and grandchildren?

3) What do you enjoy most about your children? Grandchildren?

4) What have been some of your best times with your children? Grandchildren?

5) Which of your children or grandchildren have an unusually interesting job?

6) With which of your relatives do you have a close relationship? How did this relationship develop?

7) How important is it to live near your children and/or grandchildren?

8) How important were your grandparents as you were growing up?

Who are your best friends?
Why?

"I like myself better when I am with you."
—*Unknown*

1) What qualities do you look for in a friend?

2) What friend have you known the longest? How and where did you meet?

3) When you were growing up, did your parents like your friends?

4) Describe a friend who helped you through a difficult time.

5) Describe a friend who has made you feel loved and appreciated.

6) What is it that draws you toward one person and not another?

7) Why do you think some people have a hard time making friends?

8) Do you consider your siblings among your best friends?

34
Pets

Are you a pet person?

*"Don't accept your dog's admiration as conclusive
evidence that you are wonderful."*

—*Ann Landers*

1)   Growing up, which pet was your favorite?

2)   Were pets allowed in your house?

3)   How did you handle the death of a pet?

4)   What advice would you give to someone buying a pet?

5)   Describe a favorite pet related memory.

6)   What are the advantages to owning a pet? Disadvantages?

7)   Did you ever regret owning a pet?

8)   How important is it for a child to own a pet?

9)   Over the course of your life, how many pets have you owned?

10)   How does your culture feel about owning a pet?

Unique Experiences

Kindergarten   Birth of Child   Buying a Car   Meeting in-laws

When was the first time you received a medal or award for something?

1) Do you remember owning your own car?

2) Describe the first time you saw a mountain or an ocean. How did you feel?

3) Were you the first in your family to graduate from high school or college? How did that feel?

4) What do you recall about buying your first house?

5) What do you remember about the birth of your first child?

6) What do you remember about your first job?

7) Who is the most famous person you have ever met? How did it happen?

8) Do you recall a family purchase that impacted the family in a big way (TV, boat...)?

What historic event will you never forget?

1) What was it about this event that made it so powerful?

2) Where were you and what you were doing when 9/11 took place?

3) Have you ever visited a Holocaust museum? What did you learn?

4) Have you ever participated in a demonstration? Why did you participate?

5) Do you remember a major breakthrough regarding a medical discovery?

6) Which natural disasters do you remember?

7) What were the worst weather conditions you have ever experienced?

8) How has war impacted your life?

37 🦢 Scary Stories... and then What Happened?

Drowning   *Stolen Purse*   *Choking*   *Car Accident*

> ## Have you ever had a really scary event happen to you?
> ## Tell me about it!

1) Were you ever driving too fast and your car went out of control?

2) Were you ever cooking and forgot about the food you left frying on the stove?

3) Were you ever in a lake and suddenly the water got very deep, and you didn't know how to swim?

4) Were you ever in a situation in which you thought you or someone else was going to die?

5) Were you ever in a plane that started to shake and lose altitude?

6) Were you ever pickpocketed? What were the circumstances?

7) Were you ever walking home alone at night when you heard footsteps behind you?

8) Have you ever spent a night in jail?

9) Have you ever been chased by an aggressive animal?

10) Have you ever been lost? What happened?

Fried grasshoppers   *Brain*   *Tongue*   *Pig's feet*   *Lutefisk*

Are you a person who likes to try new foods or one who sticks to what you know?

1) What is the strangest food you have ever eaten?

2) My friend likes scrambled eggs with ketchup. What odd food combinations do you enjoy?

3) What unusual or special foods did your family prepare for holidays?

4) Do you have a disaster story about cooking?

5) Of all the restaurants you have ever visited, which one stands out in your memory? Why?

6) Who in your family were exceptionally good cooks? What types of food did they prepare?

7) What is your favorite meal? Dessert?

8) Can you share a cooking tip (like the addition of a flavoring or a technique) that generally brings compliments?

Describe a time when you did something you regretted...

"Knock Knock Puddin' Head!"
Says Grandma Eileen when someone makes a poor choice!

1) If you ever bought a lemon (a defective product), how did it happen and what did you do about it?

2) Have you ever lost money gambling or investing? Explain the circumstances. What did you learn?

3) Have you ever given your credit card number to a con artist over the phone? What were you thinking?

4) Have you ever been the victim of a scam? What happened? What did you learn?

5) Have you ever been on a date you knew was a mistake?

6) Have you ever had regrets about a tattoo?

7) Have you ever left your car or your house unlocked and something valuable was stolen?

8) What life lessons have you learned from your mistakes?

Retirement Years

"When the train stops, don't say, 'Maybe next time. I'm busy now, another day perhaps. I'll be more organized. I'll have more energy. I'll surely have more cash.' There may not be another train. So when that engine stops, and friends call out to come on board, why do you hesitate? The waiting years are gone. Get on!!"

—Eileen Berger

40 ⌇ The World: Then and Now

Looking back, what inventions have made your life easier?

1) How did the purchase of a particular appliance or piece of equipment impact your family?

2) As a young person, how did you get your news?

3) How were your childhood activities different from the activities of children today?

4) What do you remember about your first car?

5) Was there a time when you thought your outfit was especially sharp? What were you wearing?

6) In what ways did the meals you ate as a child differ from the meals you eat today?

7) How has your life been impacted by advances in medicine?

8) How has the way you dress, the way you shop, and the way you travel changed over your lifetime?

9) What are the pros and cons of television and iPhones?

10) When you think about today's technology, what amazes you most?

How would you describe your retirement years?

"Age is an issue of mind over matter.
If you don't mind, it doesn't matter!"
—Mark Twain

1) How long have you been retired? Why did you retire when you did?

2) As a retiree, what has been your biggest adjustment?

3) When did you decide to sell your home?

4) How did you choose to live where you now live?

5) What do you like most about the place where you live?

6) What do you do to stay physically active?

7) What activities now fill your days?

8) How important are goals in life, especially after you retire?

9) When do you feel most alive? The happiest?

10) What new technology have you found most helpful or annoying?

Here's What I Learned

42 ❧ Reflections

At the end of the day, what is life all about?

"The art of being wise is the art of knowing what to overlook."

—*Unknown*

1) Name a personal quality for which you are thankful.

2) Who in your life has influenced you the most?

3) Who threw you a life jacket when you needed it?

4) Looking back, what are your proudest accomplishments?

5) Health and finances permitting, what would you still like to do?

6) What lights up your life?

7) What is one issue you feel strongly about?

8) When Caesar decided to cross the Rubicon River with his army, he knew there was no turning back. It could be disaster or glory. What was your Rubicon crossing?

9) What is one of the best decisions you have ever made?

Our Invitation

If Only You Would Ask is a resource to inspire quality conversation with the elderly. We would appreciate knowing how this resource works for you.

Please join us at www.ifonlyyouwouldask.com

To share your experiences using the book

To let us know what happened when you asked the questions

To order additional copies of the book

To ask your questions

To invite the authors to speak to your group

Here's wishing you many hours of enjoyable conversation!

—Eileen and Joan

About the Authors

Eileen Opatz Berger graduated from the College of St. Benedict and the University of Wis/River Falls. Presently she teaches English as a Second Language. Along with her family, foreign students have been the joy of her life. Favorite pastimes include travel, writing, and tennis. She currently divides her time between White Bear Lake, Minnesota and Sun City West, Arizona.

Joan Berger Bachman is extremely pleased and proud to be coauthoring a book with her mom! As a teenager, Joan recalls her mother's advice: "When you are in a social situation, always make an effort to ask each person three questions. This shows that you are interested in what they have to say." In other words, give people the opportunity to talk about themselves. Generally, people are pleased to share, and you will have deflected the attention from yourself. So it comes as no real surprise that four decades later, she has coauthored a book filled with questions to promote quality conversations!

Joan resides with her husband, John, in Rochester, Minnesota. Proud mother of three grown children and grandmother to five, she is grateful for family, for health, and for friends who continue to enrich her life.

CPSIA information can be obtained
at www.ICGtesting.com
Printed in the USA
BVOW11s0358200118
505525BV00012B/88/P